Dog

This is for my sister, Angela,
and my brother, René Marcel,
especially the bits about our mum.

Also by John Hegley

Glad to Wear Glasses
Can I Come Down Now, Dad?
Five Sugars Please
These Were Your Father's
Love Cuts
The Family Pack
Beyond Our Kennel

Saint and Blurry (Rykodisc CD)

JOHN HEGLEY

Dog

Methuen

Methuen

1 3 5 7 9 10 8 6 4 2

First published in Great Britain in 2000 by Methuen Publishing Limited
215 Vauxhall Bridge Road, London SW1V 1EJ

Copyright © 2000 John Hegley

John Hegley has asserted his right under the Copyright, Designs
and Patents Act, 1988, to be identified as the author of this work

Methuen Publishing Limited Reg. No. 3543167

A CIP catalogue record for this book is available from the British Library

ISBN 0 413 75560 6

Typeset by SX Composing DTP, Rayleigh, Essex

Printed and bound in Great Britain by
Creative Print and Design (Wales), Ebbw Vale

Contents

Mum and Dog

I know so little about my mother's beginnings. She was born in 1920, in Ramsgate. Her father was the proud automobile-owning postmaster of nearby Wye village, where she spent her childhood and early teens before beginning her nursing career in Whipps Cross Hospital, London. As I say, I know so little.

She told us, that on her evenings off from the hospital, she wore tight pointed shoes, which were the reason for her big toes being permanently tucked over their neighbours. She met my father at a French club, some-where in London, sometime during the war. My father had a French mother and was a native of Paris, which explains his presence in such an establishment. I suspect my mum would have been there because of the exotic image of the French. She liked to have things with a flavour of sophistication and breeding. She ended up with my father.

My Dad's mother was a French dancer, a very young bride to his own English father, who quickly abandoned the family. Grandma returned to the stage, and I feel that my mother resented her; maybe because Grandma had neglected maternal duties while making a one-parent livelihood, or maybe because she was a rival for my dad's attention, or maybe because she was horrible. Mum did, however, approve of the impressive French show business connections with Maurice Chevalier (on the stage) and 18th-century keyboard composer Jean Philippe Rameau (in the blood). My parents were married, and the newlyweds lived in a basement in Islington, where they were soon to have my brother, little René Marcel. Eight years later, when I was born, the French connection had faded, and subsequently the name selected for me was John. The flat was too small for a quartet and the move was made to Luton, where houses were easier to come by, and, where sophistication was not. My dad did not bring home a large or a full wage packet and my mother once joked that he had everything in his wallet except money. In the Luton household the best had to be made of a shoestring budget and my mother did very well. She would compare prices on supermarket shelving and shuttle between checkouts to make the ends of the shoestrings meat, two veg, and a sweet into the bargain.

We once had a photo of my mother with a nursing girlfriend in London, dolled up and ready to take on the world. In Luton, never once did my parents have a night out together. A holiday was a day out at Clacton or Bournemouth. And we had my sister now. Two years younger than me, my mum called her Precious; my brother and I did not.

In a concerted attempt to retrieve a more sophisticated status, Mum ordered the *Sunday Times* which remained virtually unread. We also acquired a Beagle, the dog of the hunting classes. He was twenty-five guineas, and we bought him in instalments. The ears came first. The creature was frighteningly ill-tempered and ripped the *Sunday Times* to ribbons as it entered the abode. He didn't like us much either, and for years lurked, lip curled, ready to go off.

I made my own contribution to the gentrification package by qualifying for the local boys' grammar school, therein taking up complimentary violin lessons. My nightly scrapings were music to my mother's ears.

There was a green outside our semi-detached bungalow which was used by the children in the council houses opposite for footballing purposes, much to the chagrin and migraine of my mother. She would stand at the window for hours at a time, waiting for the ball to approach her territory. Once an infringement had been observed, my father would be dispatched with great speed to give them a talking to, but the kids did not recognise his authority and were grossly insubordinate. It came to a head, when, on the pavement outside, they painted the phrase BOB HEGLEY IS A SEX MANIAC. I had the feeling my mother disagreed. The police were called, culprits were found and warned, and there was a brief lull in the antagonism, but the soccer season inevitably returned. When the people next door started allowing their child to join the footballers on the green I think my mum saw it as a betrayal. She'd seen the situation as a respectable home owners versus scummy council people divide; the collapse of this oversimplification contributed to our leaving the town on my father's retirement in 1970.

I am writing this in the Portobello Road, in a rooftop café. In Luton, my mother used to love old films on the telly which depicted the London streets, and she eagerly pointed out to my father recognised landmarks. Luton was a big disappointment after the big city. However, there was one source of significant joy during this wilderness sojourn. Football had become my mother's ruin. But also through football would come a fabulous fulfilment. I had started to take an interest in the Town's football side after England's World Cup victory in '66. Being despised at school, I quickly clicked into soccer as a source of engagement, and my mum supported my support with growing fervour. Together we would watch for away results on the telly and leap from the three-piece seating if 'The Town' were announced to be the victors in a meeting.

Later I would attend many of these games, and it was through this travel that I would get a taste for the north of England, Bradford in particular, where I would later take up a university place. Getting the fares together for this jaunting was daunting on my mother's budget, but she always managed it. She would see excursions advertised weeks in advance and would ask me such questions as 'Do you want to go to Barrow, John?' An act of massive and total giving, the essence of parenthood. Home games I always attended and any match I went to would be followed by a detailed and impassioned debriefing on my return. She got to know the individual players' profiles intimately. The intimacy was always a knowing from afar. She never entered a football ground in her life, but many she entered in her imagining, and I believe that she and I were significantly responsible for Luton winning the Fourth Division Championship at the height of our involvement in 1968. The night they received the trophy we danced around the living room. Any boisterous activity in the home usually moved Hunter to barking and biting, but this time he was shut into grudging quietude as Mum and I festivalled like crazy; and she with the ribbons of *Sunday Times* fluttering from her now greying hair.

Thus was affected the miraculous turnabout of the fortunes of the Hatters, although I'm not sure how deeply she believed in the miracles of the Catholicism to which she converted on marrying my father. She did not attend communion. I do not know whether there was some unforgivable sin at the root of this or whether she just preferred her bread leavened and with marmalade. She did believe in miracles though. One ferociously cold winter she was out shopping, desperate for paraffin for the oil heater. But everywhere had sold out. She had walked the whole town through, and was reaching desperation, when she was, as she told us intently on her return, approached by a couple of 'old dears'. Old dear was a term she applied pityingly to the more ancient of her gender. The pair in question, seeing the anguish in my mother's face, had asked if they could help. She explained her paraffin problem, and they directed her to a pet shop, telling her to enquire within. Doubting, but desperate, she followed the tip. It was a good one. The unlikely product was shockingly in stock and at a good price. Hurrying out to thank the old dears, she found them to be gone. They could have just walked on their way of course, but my mother believed they had de-materialised – phantoms or angels of some sort, whose mission had been to help her in her search to fuel her funnel.

When we left Luton behind, my brother remained: a boy no longer, and established in his airport employ. I have retained links of my own with the town, seeing virtue which was not apparent to me then. Largely unsung, the town is an underdog and I like to stroke it, but my mum was glad to be out of the place – for her it was a dog best buried.

In Bristol, there was no oppressing child footballing, there was a new freehold and there was a new lease of living for my mother. Her hair was dyed dark by the cheerful hairdresser who visited the house, and she began

5

going out in the evenings with my dad, although not in pointed footwear. She got a job inspecting brassieres for Marks and Spencers, and she got a car.

The passing of her driving test took some doing, the sort of thing that might make page 8 in the tabloids. I reckon she had about a hundred lessons and was tested maybe 15 times. There was a regular ritual of her getting sorted out in the morning for the next attempt at the test, with my father giving reassurances of her behind-the-wheel ability. He was always enormously supportive of Mum. He said that she was beautiful, he said she had a wonderful singing voice, he said she was very intelligent, he said she made lovely dinners, he said she was an excellent driver. As I say, this last one took some proving. She would leave home for the examination, bolstered by my father's enthusiasm and she would reappear through the door a couple of hours later, her confidence rattled once again by her latest failure. But then one day it was her keys we heard rattling as she returned up the path, the signal and symbol of a driver fully fledged. She had passed the examination, my father's appraisal finally vindicated.

My mother's Austin Mini was sprayed gold and we were told that she was to prepare herself for the advanced test. She never actually proceeded, but, no matter, it was nice to think that such a thing was possible. Monday to Friday, my dad would do the housework and she would return home, keys a-jangle with glad and gossipy tales of the womenfolk in the factory. She would joke about the character across the way who wore hot pants in spite of being the wrong side of the menopause. London scenes on the television drew only casual recognition now. The *Sunday Times* had been stopped. The *Sun* newspaper was now purchased for the bingo, rather than the kudos. Airs and graces were gone. She was enjoying herself. At 52 my mother was in her West Country hayday.

In 1973 I left for university. Soon after my sister left to make a new home with her husband. Mum and Dad sold up the bricks and mortar and bought a mobile home on a nearby residential site. They bought it outright. It cost 30 pounds. Into the smaller home a smaller dog was welcomed. Yorkie. Yorkie, the yappy Yorkshire Terrier, who would light-footedly leap on to my mother's lap and sit there happily panting, his exercise regime completed once more. Newspaper and flesh remained unbroken, all hint of Hunterdom had gone.

I recall a comical incident with my mother in the mobile home, which I believe to be a significant pointer to her personality. I had been doing some pictures of musical mice, whom I had collectively called Micetroes. For a bit of fun, I asked her for a contribution and she drew me a trio of little figures with various instruments. 'They're great, Mum,' I announced, feeling genuinely happy and privileged to see her drawings for the first time in a lifetime. She shook her head, took back the pictures, added some writing and handed them back, with the following caption appended: THREE BLIND MICE DRAWN BY A BLIND ARTIST.

When my sister had her first child, Mum showed her the ropes and the strings of infant nursing; passing away, soon after, aged 65, having done her last maternal duty, and having bloomed late in life. It was the right time to leave us. She would never have wanted to become an 'old dear'.

Mad Mum

You're pushing a pram
and you say, 'my little baby'.
You're pushing a pram, and your baby is a doggie.
You're pushing a pram
and you're also pushing eighty.
You're pushing a pram
and you like to be called a lady.
You're actually a man
and that's no problem, baby,
and it's once around the park
about a hundred times a day.
And you can be mummy
the way you want to be.
You can be mummy,
any way you want to be.
You can be mummy,
I'm just glad that you're not my mummy.

An Owner's Complaint

I've got a dog that's more like a carrot
than a dog.
It's hairy,
but only very slightly,
it has no personality to speak of,
no bark to bark of,
no head,
no legs,
no tail,
and it's all orange
and crunchy.

Dog's Dinner

There I was all done up like the dinner of a dog
but I wasn't the one you wanted.
I placed myself in front of you
but you didn't even fancy a taste,
what a waste of my presentational expertise.
I did myself up,
because I thought you were great,
I did myself up
put myself on a plate,
I did myself up,
but it was inappropriate.
I was ready to eat
like a hearty party special treat for Rover,
I had made up my mind
I was laid on the line
but you just stepped over it.
You weren't in the mood,
for being in the nude
and you weren't in the mood
for dog food.
I wanted the feel
of your lips and your tongue
but I wasn't the kind of meal
you wanted to get your teeth in and among.
I was very keen,
but you didn't want me in your intestine,
I did myself up, like a doggie's dinner
I did myself up but I wasn't a winner

I did myself up, and it was inappropriate.
Even with the Winalot,
even with the Chockie Drops
it wasn't chocks away,
this dog's dinner didn't have its day.
No day.

Pear-shaped

The first night me and you went out
we came out of the bar
and I cast my eyes to the heavens
and said, 'God, if you're up there, ta!'
Me and you were going to the Dog Star
as far as I could tell,
I thought you were the dog's testicles
and the other bit as well.
I couldn't Adam and Eve it,
I thought I had escaped,
but we bit into the apple
and it all went pear-shaped.
Pear-shaped, pear-shaped,
it all went shaped like a pear,
It was shaping up so nicely,
but we didn't actually get there.
I was more attached to you
than to Match of the Day,
I thought it was sorted
as they say.
Bravas, bravas, potatas bravas, yeah!
It all seemed brave potato-shaped
then it all went shaped like a pear.
I had so much baggage and you were such a case,
we never even made it into outer space,
let alone to the Dog Star.
I thought we were going to be going strong
but you were a right one

and I was wrong
and it all went pear-shaped, pear-shaped,
still I don't despair,
knees up Mother Theresa,
let's see your underwear.

The Absence of Dogs

The absence of dogs – the surface of Mars.
The absence of dogs – the penalty shoot-out.
The absence of dogs – the Popemobile.
The absence of dogs – the beloved who left him because
The absence of dogs – the man alone with his best friend
                        who is a man.
The absence of dogs –
the undog.
the ultimately sprog,
the dog beyond further shrinking
a dog that is only a dog in my thinking,
a dog that can log on
and bog off
all in one mothball.

The Reluctant

I do want you
but were I to have you
then I would want you less,
and I want to want you infinitely.
If I never have you, I never lose you.
Please
excuse
the mess.

Usk

There was a young woman of Usk
whose teeth had a tinge of the tusk;
they were glowing and white
and a whale of a sight
but not quite so impressive at dusk.

Gwent

There once was a woman of Gwent
who was useless at pitching a tent;
she hammered a peg
through a bone in her leg
and immediately after, she went
AAAAARGHH!

Classic

In the radio interview
the former Classics student
asked me about the similarity between
my writings and those of Aristotle.
I said I didn't know there was such a similarity.
When she asked how useful my Sociology Degree had
    been,
I answered that it had taught me how to felt-tip
my idea of a potato on to a sheet of transparent plastic,
then compare it with the real world
by placing it over an existing potato,
and she said, 'that's Plato'.

Questions of Poetry

Does poetry need to rhyme?
Poetry needs to bleed.

What is poetry?
Poetry is the wounding and the healing,
the conscience, the pain and the stain upon the ceiling.

Where is poetry?
Roly-poly,
wear and tear,
poetry is everywhere, friend.

The Flat Cap's Secret

I bought it for one pound fifty
and I thought it was nifty
but it was not,
because included in the price
was a colony of lice.

The Drop of the Hats

There was a time when Luton was the proud
hatmaker to the crowd,
straw boaters a notable speciality.
It's aviation and car production now,
the milliner's trade has had to bow to fashion's villainy.
They still call the football team the Hatters
but it's more a matter of dreaming now:
in and not *on* the head.
Luton thrived when you touched your hat.
Now a straw is something to be clutched at.

The Luton Riots Revisited

Grandpa Ted's gone up to bed
and he's sleeping tight and fast,
when in the road outside his home
he's heard a fright'nin' blast,
and he's pressed against the window pane
and poor old Grandpapa
sees the kids are having fun
with matches and his car.

And Grandpa's thrown his hands up,
he's thrown them in the air,
one goes up with disbelief
the other with despair,
it's enough to make old Grandpa
take his hands to his own hair
and rip it right out by the roots
but he ain't got none to spare.

And Grandpa Ted reflects upon
his home town's downward slide,
from Eric Morecambe's patronage
to the shenanigans outside;
from the former fame in the millinery game,
giving the world its boaters,
to a summer's night of setting light
to the bonnets of Vauxhall motors.

And Grandpa he'd decided
it's his duty to go down,
and in the doorway of his dwelling place
he's spoken with renown
'You didn't need to riot when I was a lad
you had the bleeding war,
but if you have to riot
can you keep it quiet
it's twenty-five to four.'

Dame

Witter witter
nag nag
glittering handbag,
there's only just the one of us in any one show
with a pair of beach-ball bosoms
and a lot of innuendo,
with lipstick up to the nostrils
and right down to our chins:
the acceptable face
of the cross-dressed sin.

Game for the Pajamas

Mr Callow and Co.
burned a lot of tallow
adding new light
to this old entertainment,
then came the mixed press
which pressed against the fledgling flame
and blew against success.
It's a shame,
it's a good game,
if a little relentless,
and I much enjoyed the taking part
as well as taking the money,
even if I was described
as 'dismally unfunny'.
(*The Telegraph*)

Rhyl

A playful young woman of Rhyl
made a plateful of rarebit for Bill,
but Bill couldn't cope,
it was slices of soap
on a facecloth put under the grill.
He said to her, 'I do not care
for this manner of toiletry fare,
I don't like the taste
or the concept of waste',
but he had to admit it was rare.

Toronto Haiku

Under the scraped sky
I'm a drop in the metropo-
-lis. City zen.

The Death of the Potatoes

In the monastery kitchen
my job has been to sort out the potatoes.
On the shelves overhead,
the broad serving plates
and the hoard of diminishing saucepans.
The brown jackets
I have removed religiously.
Fist tight-shut around the cord-bound tool,
I have revealed their inner selves,
cutting and gouging wherever required.
Once peeled and poked eyeless
I have quartered them
and commended them to the heat
and the slaughter
upon the stove.
I kneel beneath the steaming.
My eyes are streaming.
Brother Matthew enters.
He questions my pose.
I tell him, I pray for the souls of the potatoes.

Je regrette quelque chose

I regret
never having found the net
for a professional football team;
I would have liked to
but occasionally I do it in my dreaming.

I don't regret
no longer having my boyhood
clockwork steam
train set;
it is marvellous in my memory.

I don't regret
not cross-dressing in fishnet
when I was seventeen, before my beard came;
it's a shame but never mind.

I don't regret
Bet Lynch leaving Coronation Street,
she was good but so was her innings.
I don't regret
never having placed a lottery bet
in spite of what my winnings might have been.

I do regret rather
never having had the chance
to go to France
with my father,
getting settled in a bar
perhaps with Monsieur Cantona
and my Dad needs no translator
and he's joking with the waiter
and we all play football later.

The Law According to Neck

Our French master was given the nickname
of Neck,
because he was blessed
with a heck of a distance
between the bottom of his face
and the top of his chest.
When we were marking our neighbour's vocabulary test,
Neck would always lay down
very specific guidelines for the task,
these he referred to as his four simple rules:
if it's not right, it's wrong
if it's not there, it's wrong
if you can't read it, it's wrong
and if it's not wrong, it's right.

Unacceptable Social Exchange

Recently, in a public lavatory, I had just finished having a wee, when a young man holding a sleeping toddler came and stood in the urinal stall beside me. With only one hand free, he could not get the necessary purchase on his zip and I asked if he would like me to do it for him. The man became defensive. I had apparently crossed the line between assistance and interference. There are times, however, when unsolicited help is unlikely to be refused. The person running for a bus will not complain if you keep it waiting for them, although they will if you ask them for financial reward. And rightly so, no contract has been entered into. The person who asks someone for directions and gets no joy will not usually mind if you say you overheard them asking and can help. If you say you overheard them asking and cannot help either they will be less grateful.

Certain information, although appropriate, can still be unwelcome. I once heard a chap in a bar asking a friend about a tonic for haemorrhoids. I excused my eaves-dropping and listed four or five excellent creams and ointments as well as an old remedy using herbs placed in a saucepan of boiling water, which you then sat upon. Before I got on to explaining that care should be taken not to overfill the vessel, I was silenced by the irritated sufferer, who funnily enough was the same bloke I'd met in the public lavatory.

Me Poem

me
me
me
me ME
me
Me me *me*
Me
me
me
me
Me
me
me me
Me me
Me me me ME Me
Me
me ME
me
Me me *me*
Me

Me
me
me me
Me me me
Me me me me. ME me Me
Me me

ME
me
   me
      ME me me me me
me me me me me me me,
me
mE Me
that's enough about me.

Knee Poem

Once when I was in a shopping centre
I banged my knee
and I went,
'Aah, m'knee,
m'knee!'
And someone gave me
some m'ney.

Tree Poem

The leaves
have all left,
but the tree
will be
all right.

Bee Poem

I'm stripey and I'm wipey
when I'm visiting the flowers.
I dust and dive,
my wings sing buzz
for hours and ours
is a happy old hive.
I live in a colony
and I like to get all polleny.

Key Poem

Being a key
is my curse.
I live on a ring,
in a purse
or a pocket
rarely seeing my true home.
Only for a moment,
when I unlock it.

Sea Poem

The shallows
the deeps
the blues and
the greens,
the seaweed
and the submarines,
the nautical,
the net,
the yards of yachts
and lots and lots
and lots and lots and lots and lots and lots and lots and
lots and lots
of wet.

Key and Pea Poem

Even though keys and peas sound similar,
it is very hard to unlock a door with a pea,
and a bunch of keys is not very tasty,
even with plenty of tomato sauce.

Flea Poem

Dog's back.
Itch
itch
scratch
scratch
scratch
scratch
scratch
scratch
pause

itch
scratch
scratch
itch
paws
scratch
scratch
scratch
scratch
scratch
scratch
scratch
scratch
scratch
scratch scratch scratch
bald patch.

Cup of tea poem

 Tea

 Tea

 Tea

Tea

Empty

Freddie Four Legs

Hello, I'm Freddie Four Legs,
I've got more legs than you.
I've got more than what is normal legs
and I've got four feet too.
When I'm in a shoe shop
I don't just buy a pair
and when I ride my bicycle
there's two legs going spare.
But this is not the problem,
it's the people who call out
inflammatory comments
that I complain about.
They just see what is wrong with me
they're just not being fair
they've never seen my brilliant impression of chair.
Most days I can take it
but there's times I take it bad,
especially when the nasty comments
came from Mum and Uncle.
But, then looking on the brighter side,
the mocking's a good job:
while they make fun of all my legs
they miss my massive gob.

Santa Fantasy

This can be read aloud, leaving words in capitals for listeners to guess

Santa's not a doggie
and he hasn't any paws,
Santa's not a cat
although I know that
he has CLAUS.
There's many a house he's been to
where mince pies have disappeared,
he picks them up and puts them
through a big hole in his BEARD.
He clambers down the chimneys
with his famous bulging sack,
it's always much more difficult
when he is climbing BACK.
Sometimes Santa's miserable
and sometimes he's upset:
some folk just want Santa Claus
for all that they can GET.
The colour of his costume
matches Rudolf's runny nose
and one year just for fun
he'll bring a sackful of potaTOES.
Santa's got another name,
a saint's name, it's Saint Nicholas,
he's got one for his beard as well;
he says it is RIDICHOLAS.

The Big Brown Paper Bag

It's very very long
and it is also very wide,
it's not the sort of paper bag
that's usually supplied,
you could fit the world's biggest dog inside
with room for its tail to wag,
what is it?
It's the big brown paper bag.

Filled with over a hundred bananas
the sides still wouldn't split,
if you're looking for a hiding place
then this could well be it,
now, it may not be quite big enough to play a game of
    tag
but it's still pretty big,
it's the big brown paper bag.

Peter the Piece of String

He was snipped off a big ball of string
like a baby is snipped from its Mum,
but he didn't need any milk because he was already fully
    grown.
He went to school straight away in somebody's pocket
but he never learned anything except how to swing a
    conker.
He didn't want to be a conker bonker all this life though,
so he made an announcement,
'hey, what if all us bits of string got together?
We could stretch even further than a ball of string could
and each piece would still be itself.'
But all the other pieces of string were scared of big
    changes.
Only one piece from his conker days agreed to get tied up
    with him,
and though they could stretch that little bit further,
Peter often dreamt of what it would be like if all the
    various bits of string got together.
But they never.

What a Poem's Not

A poem is not an Ant
but it can be quite short.
A poem is not a Banana
but there may be something under its skin.
A poem is not a Coat
but it may have some warmth in it.
A poem is not a Dog
but it might be quite a friend.
A poem is not an Endless pair of trousers
but it can be quite long.
A poem is not a Football shaped like a cucumber.
A poem is not a Great number of things.
A poem is not a Hedgehog
but it might be hard to get hold of.
A poem is not an Igloo
but it can feel like home.
A poem is not a Jumble sale,
but it might contain some rubbish.
A poem is not a Kite
but it might enjoy the wind.
A poem is not a Lightbulb
but you can change it if you want to.
A poem is not a Monkey
but it can be quite human.
A poem is not a Nut
but you can give it to a monkey.
A poem is not an opera score or an open sore
but it can be revealing.

A poem is not a Prison
and it shouldn't feel like one either.
A poem is not a Question . . .
actually it is sometimes.
A poem is not a Radio
but you may have to tune into it.
A poem is not a Slot machine
but you may have to put something into it.
A poem is not a Toothbrush
So don't clean your teeth with it.
A poem is not an Umbrella
but it can give you protection.
A poem is not a Verruca
and I'm glad.
A poem is not a Wig
but maybe it will change you.
A poem is not an X-ray:
make no bones about it.
A poem is not a Year-old bag of vegetables
bit it can smell quite strongly.
A poem is not a Zylophone
and it can spell words wrongly.

Country Tony

Whenever Tony saw a cat or a dog
darting undercover
he would say 'Look, a badger!'
One day when Miss was talking about sheep and cattle
Tony put up his hand and said that he lived on a farm
and his father drove a combine harvester.
We were all very impressed
and Miss expressed to the rest of us
what a combine harvester was.
A month later, after the parents' evening
and a talk with Tony's parents,
she announced that the boy had been lying.
He actually lived in council accommodation
and his father had no job at all,
although apparently they did have a pet badger
and a combine harvester.

Bird

Tony gives John a book about Charlie Parker.
He looks a bit like Tony, but a fair bit darker.
John has never heard
of Bird
(which is the nickname of Charlie).
The book is a book of stories from people who knew
  him.
John reads the stories without knowing Bird's song.
A sort of faith.
A faith that his friend will only give him
what is necessary.
The stories create inquisitive ears,
but not for ten years will he buy a recording of the great
  man.
And why does he buy then?
John does not know.
Just like he does not know the face of the moon
from the vantage of New Zealand.

P.S. Who's got my Charlie Parker book?

Doggèd Love

He's seen the one he'd like to share
his bone with
but experience has shown
it cannot last,
he's weighed it very carefully
and knows that it is best
if he walks past.
He will not lick the place his tongue would lead him.
He will not smell
the spell that would be cast.
He will not come into the sacred circle
because he knows that it is only without having
that he hast.

Spot the Genuine Australian Saying

He couldn't hit a hanky
if he blew his nose in it.
He couldn't wear a pair of glasses
even if he was wearing them.
He couldn't be of help even if he was giving assistance.
He couldn't tell his belovèd that he loved her.
He couldn't get a soapy stick
up a dog's bum.

Say it Now

Don't hold on till it's time to go
before you let your emotional side show,
don't hold on until tomorrow,
don't hold on for another moment.
Saying I love you's not original
but nor is never letting someone know.
Why leave it till it's almost time to say the last goodbye
before you get to say the big hello?
Don't hang on till the gate is closing,
don't hang on till the daisies grow.
Why wait until it's nearly far too late,
why wait for another moment?
Do you feel at home with a heart that's hardly ever open?
Why keep it bottled up
when there's a genie hoping to get out
to shout it out,
the thing you really should have spoken about by now
why keep it bottled up until that heart is broken?
One wish: no feeling will dilly-dally.
One wish: no lagging with love to show.
One wish: don't be an emotional scallywag
or a silly so-and-so.
Say it now, it's not a moment too soon,
Say it now, don't wait until next July or June.
Say it now, don't wait for the next eclipse of the moment.
Say it now, give up on the muting,
Say it now, do a bit of re-routing,
don't go living in Slough
when you could be living in Luton
Town.

More Need

I need you like a circus needs a clown
I need you like a dog called Domestos
needs to be put down
the toilet.
I need you like Luton needs Town
I need you like Palace needs Crystal
like Rovers and City need Bristol,
do you get my gist?
Just in case you don't
I'll continue with the list.
I need to be kissed
I need you to find me hard to resist
I need you to want to hold my hand.
I need you like sandpaper needs wood to nuzzle
I need you like a dot-to-dot puzzle
needs more than one dot
unless it is not
to be taken particularly seriously.

The cat

The flat cat

knows

Nothing

The Eventful Walkies

I was out a stretching my old barker in the park one day
when this woman came walking from the other way with
   another one.
Both dogs were off the leash and running
and I thought she was stunningly attractive.
The woman not the dog,
which had just got interactive with my own.
'Don't they get on well!' I said,
'And I like your two-tone shell-suit, by the way.'
She said, 'it's a tracksuit.'
I said, 'oh, I'm sorry.'
She said, 'you can come round to my place
and I'll let you see my shell-suit
and you can smell it, if you fancy.'
And I said, 'that sounds Nancy.'
I really meant another word
but couldn't recollect it at the time.
And then our dogs ran on to the soccer pitch
and the air was all of a sudden chock-a-block
with fornication-rich lingo, of the go away variety.

The players were swearing because of our dogs' daring
to invade their football patch.
The match official
blew the tiny plea
around his shiny whistle
and I shouted, 'why don't you take their names and stick
   them in your notebook!'

The other jogging dog-owners thought me funny and
    clever
but the players never,
and they took it on themselves to give chase.
The ref joined in the race.

Later round the other jogger's place,
as she was patching up my face,
it all got fairly intimate.
She said, 'come round again will you,
here's my address.'
I said, 'but I know your address now . . .'
She merely reiterated, 'here's my address,
and next time I won't be wearing one.'
And I said,
'Can I see your shell-suit now?'

More Drawing

She told me I could draw. I said I can't draw, and she said you can no more not draw than you cannot draw breath.

Mr Hotel

Hello Mr Hotel
we've trundled up by train
we're looking forward to our break
could you take a moment to explain,
we've got your little brochure
with the room rates at the back,
please tell us Mr Hotel,
are we on the right track?
Is it true?
It's three nights bed and breakfast
for the price of two?
It's true?
Yippie aye-ooh!

Thank you Mr Hotel
I've come up here to spend
some time in these grand surroundings
with my brand new friend,
now it says here on the notice
leave your keys at the reception.
Is there any chance at all that you could make me an
    exception?
You see I get such comfort, from knowing I've got my
    key.
And is there any possibility,
that I could call you Mummy? . . .

. . . Let's leave that for a moment,
what we would like to do
is build a dog from the furniture
that we find in the room,
you see, we two are artists
our bags are full of tools
it's my first weekend with my new friend
I hope you'll bend the rules.
You will . . . But you won't be able to do
three nights for the price of two?
I think we'll leave the furniture.

Maybe we'll go
out into the snow
and make a dog from the snow
but before we go making a start,
can we take just the smallest part,
just a splinter of the furniture,
just a splinter, for its winter heart?
It's OK with you?
Yippie aye-oooh!

The Snowman's Dog

Up in Grange-over-Sands
we had love on our hands
and with gloves on hands we went out in the snow
and we moulded and melded a dog from the snow
and then on our back paws
we both went back indoors
and went up to the man at the desk
and I asked of him, 'hey did you know
there's a dog sitting out in the snow?'
and the man at the desk, he said, 'oh!'
and he went and he opened a window
and he spoke to the dog in the snow
he said, 'snow dog you haven't a kennel,
snow dog you haven't a flannel
for wiping the tears that will flow.'
We left him and went up the stairs
and we sat on our chairs
and looked down on the dog from our window,
and with night drawing in
we began drawing him,
the dog, not the man down below,
which appeared on the snow of our pages,
out of the lead of our pencils,
and yours was 2B
and mine was 2B,
and I said we were 2B together,
and you told me 2B quiet.

Yes?

I notice you are beautiful
I see that you are neat.
Is everything complete?
Or are you lacking
something me-shaped?

No

I want to inform you that
BETRAY
is an anagram of
BYE RAT.

It's bust.
More than rust.
It's not that to which I'll readjust.
It's dust.

What gets me is the decimated trust.
It's the lies, not the lust.

Alright, it is the lust a bit.

No No
(A 17 Syllable Message for February the 14th)

Dear

Oh dear,

You filthy swine.
Please don't be my Valentine.

No love.
None.

The Bob-a-Job Job

The job involved completing the securing of her shed in case of high wind. We were shown a dangle of cable, which she explained she had already fastened round the other side. The cable was as thick as your finger and the hole she got us to dig for it was as deep as a grave, and the piece of wood for the fastening was the size of a moderate tree trunk.

The final and most difficult part involved stretching the wire and winching it around a heavy-duty pin which she had us hammer into the upright. It was a big job, but she directed the operation with efficiency.

When we had finished we went round the other side of the shed and noticed that the cable was not attached to another post, it was merely hooked on to the side of the shed, so our work was of no use in the anchoring sense whatsoever.

If You Can't Get Love

If no one wants to know your secrets.
If you've got nobody to whisper your name.
If night time brings no kissing.
If the game of life is missing
that vital ingredient,
there is help at hand.
If you're aching for the big affection,
the one that brings those pennies falling
from the clouds above,
if you can't get love:
put your hand into an oven glove.

If you want something really beautiful
how about some steak and kidney pies?
Throw in your lot
with some hot jacketed potatoes,
there's no looking back
when you've taken out their eyes.
If you can't get love
start cooking,
those blues won't get a look in,
make it warm and make it tasty,
make some flaky pastry.
If you can't get love, you mustn't grumble,
can't you hear your tummy rumble?
If you can't get love, get out of bed
you can roly poly in the kitchen instead
and instead of mixing souls

mix with mixing bowls,
who needs love when you're kneading bread?
If you can't get love
put your head in the oven.

Misery

I'm not a cheerful person
I'm not a happy guy
I feel like a piece of muck in the eye
of the universe,
people say things could be worse
but they're lying.

Life's like a cream doughnut,
without any cream
and without
any doughnut.

Your Journey

I helped to make you what you are
and now you need to be it on your own.
However far you go, I know
the further you will go away from me.
If I still see you then,
then I will see the world
you've hurled towards
and curled towards
is not a part of me.
Your journey is your own
and you are starting out alone,
my heart is like a stone
and yet I know how it must be.
I know you must be
free.
(And I knew you wouldn't get very far without me.)

The Ant in the Art Gallery

The art is not really for the ant,
it is very much above her head
and even if it were lower
it would have little bearing on the six-legged life.
The pictures were made before pain
was a cliché in artistic circles.
How much the ant can know of pain
we cannot know.
I am writing this in the Joan Miró exhibition in
    Barcelona.
I am in the café.
I frequently prefer the gallery café
to the gallery.
I think the ant might like it in here too.

The Difficult Tooth

My dentist filled me in on the problem
with the aid of a diagram.
Watching him at work,
I hoped he was better at dentistry
than he was at art.

The Art of Advertising

Ladies and businessmen,
it is unlikely
that any reference
to your bank or beer,
or whatever,
will appear
in the finished commercial.
Not even by clever implication.
Your product is merely a starting point
providing finance
for fine art.
Let this be your reward.
Art cannot afford
to set its purpose
to the increase of corporate profile or profit.
Indeed the artist may see fit
to advertise a rival product
on your account
to suit some compositional need.
Yes – we guarantee to induce *no* increase in your sales,
because the way the work is done
there will be no way of telling
which product it is you're selling:
no logo, no catchphrase
no process of suggestion,
no glorification of consumerism
or the market economy whatsoever,
art has higher things in mind,

to be doing well
it must be ill-defined
the *BIG* in ambiguity.
Let the artist choose.
You have nothing to lose
but your money.

The Price of Art in Luton

On the bridge approaching the railway,
the man was begging.
I said draw me a dog
and I'll give you a quid.
So I gave him some paper
and he did.
And I said, there you go, mate,
you can make money out of art!
Will you sign it?
As I handed him the one pound thirty-odd
I had in my pocket,
he informed me that the signed ones were a fiver.

The Sock-knack Knackered

In the absence of a hunt
the horrible Hunter
used to pilfer my brother's socks,
all stiff with stink,
and then sit guarding them, gloweringly growly
beneath the sink or the table:
a poor substitute for a ripped fox,
but it's all in the wanting,
and we always wanted them back.

If any of us kids came near,
Hunter would rear up with gnashing of teeth.
My dad was proud of being able
to command the dog to give up its plunder,
it was all in the shared glaring:
he could stare the dog into submitting
with his un-witting, un-socking looking.
But then one day my dad lost his eye,
in the sense of his ability to out-eyeball the dog, I mean,
he didn't actually *lose* his eye.
He lost his hand.

The Enemies of Dance

Start swinging at a party
and you'll find us in your space.
Life's not a dance it's a race.
Some of us can dance ourselves
but we don't relax,
we are the egomaniacs
and the stiflingly enthusiastic,
we are the television
the law
the self-conscious
and the sick on the dance floor:
We are the unavoidable,
void of any grace
we are the enemies of dancing
and we own the place.

The Sad Usherette

Last night I heard a song about an usherette
who missed the ends of all the films.
It was a catalogue
of the celebrated denouements unknown to her.
In the last verse
setting up a rhyme for 'ire',
she says (I paraphrase), I don't know any of the endings
of the films, I think I'll just . . .
and I thought the last word would be enquire
but it was retire.

The Long-standing Trainspotter

The loco pulls in with a smoke-swilling lumber,
and I make a note of its infinite number
I'm very excited, my hand is unsteady
and then I remember I've got it already.

Transport for All

The bus means more space
and less dirty,
I thought as I boarded a 30,
but I found it a feat
to get half of a seat
without somebody getting all shirty.
It seems that some people have trouble
with seats that are meant to be double,
they don't want to budge
and they treat you like sludge
just because you've got sick in your stubble.

An Introduction to Folk

There's those who'd have you keep
folk songs for the sheep.
I shared such an aspersion
until I heard a version
of a ballad by the name
of Anachie Gordon
done by one Nic Jones.
John Peel it was
who brought me to them,
the lingering longing
in the wavering tones
over intricate patterns
of the fingering bones,
since then many folk songs have moistened my eye,
and I can see why
the Morris dancer sports a spare hanky.

Gladly Bamboozled

It was early in old Alicante
just after Easter was through,
someone had said that the shops would be shut
but they didn't say what would ensue.
I took in the early May morning
I was out there and after a brew
and I noticed that people were hanging about,
with sticks of bamboo.
At first there were only a few,
but the numbers grew steadily.
Your average stick was the length of a staff
with what looked like some Christmas tree stuffed in the
  crown
and I noticed a definite movement away from the town
up the hill
and I wondered about the significance,
in fact I am still wondering about it
and I like it this way,
I like not having a clue
about the bamboo.

Domino Dotty

'Twas down the Victoria Palace Theatre
and I had mislaid my keys,
they may have gone into a cranny backstage
and so I had got down on my knees.
I shone my light into the crevice
and some keys were lit up in the shine.
And I eased them out, using a stick of bamboo
and I straight away knew they weren't mine.
Mine were attached to a domino,
by coincidence so too were these
but these had a total of five dots embossed
whereas mine had a couple of threes.
On the back of the black it said STOREROOM
it was painted in ochre and blue,
I'd noticed the door on occasions before
but on none had I ever gone through.
And inside the storeroom, do you know what I found?
Bamboo.
A lot of bamboo.

The Waggy Wedding

Me and my doggie we're going to get married in chapel,
me and my doggie are going to get wed in a while,
I'm going to take my doggie for a walk up the aisle.
Me and my doggie we're going to get married in chapel
we're going to keep it quiet, we don't want any grief from
   the fuzz,
my daddy won't be coming, they'll have to dig him up if
   he does.
My doggie won't be wearing a veil,
anyway, my doggie is male,
not that I am big on regalia determined by gender.

I hope and I pray
that it'll go OK
and not go the way
of a friend of mine
who married his doggie the other day
and then ran away
with the one who was taking the photos.
One snapper for another.
One snapper for another snapper.

Me and my doggie we're going to get married in chapel
our wedding photos are something I am dying to see,
Me and my doggie we're going to get married in chapel,
all we've got to do is get the vicar to agree.

Luton at Christmas Time

The Lord he was born in a stable
because it was full at the inn
and Luton are very low down in the table
because they're unable
to win.

Shrove Tuesday Poem

Pancake
Overkill
Every
March

Look Dad

Now, changing water into wine
can win you many a chum
and arguing with Pharisees is fine
and letting people know that all possessions are for scum
is all part of the message that is mine
(all mine)
but without a doubt the aspect of the job that's most
    appealing
over and above the faith and healing of the lepers
is to step astride the lovely loverly sea,
oh I'm ever so at home
when I am plodding on the foam
walking on the water is God's gift to me.

Raising Lazarus is good for raising profile,
and multiplying fishes may be swell
but I'd rather be in motion on the wavy pavy ocean
I've a liking for the hiking on the sea
(oh, let me tell you).
Your Sunday morning resurrections
and your rolling away stones
are not a patch on strolling over Davy Jones's locker,
I'm a shocker on my sea leg, believe me,
how I like to see 'em stare
quand je me promène sur la mer
walking on the water
walking on the water
walking on the water

is the one for me
and my doggie
(go fetch my halo, Judas).

'No more tiddlywinks, thanks!'

A Pack of Lies

There once was a woman of Frome
who went for a ride on a broom
and a wizard who took
a look up from his book
found it ever so hard to resume.

The one he'd seen sweeping the sky
with the ease of a thing that could fly
she had struck him with awe,
he was struck even more,
when some bird muck came down in his eye.

To be true what the little bird did
landed not on the eye, but the lid
and the eye was his third
but he wasn't deterred
by the splash that came in with a skid.

The wizard he went very soft
on the one he'd seen flying aloft
and he rang up his mum
who was doing a sum
she was thinking of buying a croft.

'What do I have of a chance?
Am I worth to her more than a glance?
I liken my plight
to a medieval knight
with a matchstick opposed to a lance.'

'I feel she is full of intrigue,
I feel it, till I feel fatigue',
he entered a gloom,
was the woman of Frome
in a totally different league?
In fact did she play football at all?

He felt like a man on the moon
whose planet's become a balloon
and he's just seen it burst
and he knows he's the first
and there's none'll come later or soon.

They happened to meet at a dance,
which the music was there to enhance,
she told him he moved
like a dog, she approved,
and he felt she had lowered her lance.

The witchery woman of Frome
said 'won't you come back to my room?'
The wizard said, 'yes',
and he brought up a mess,
he had never been up on a broom stick.

There was sickness all over his face,
he said, 'I am such a disgrace,'
she said, 'I agree
but it don't bother me,
you're a dirty old dog aren't you basically.'

They cleaned him up nicely and neat
then she gave him some toothpaste to eat,
he had a good rinse
and he felt like a prince,
and tied tinsel round one of his feet.

This tinsel it came from a tree
in the flat she was sharing with three
novice nuns, one of whom
would complain when the broom
wasn't where it would usually be.

The wizard said, 'please pardon me
for the tinsel I've took from your tree:
we ought to respect
what another had decked,'
and the witch said, 'correct, but it'll be
the Epiphany in a couple of minutes so don't worry
    about it.'

'The tree will be soon coming down
there's already a lot on the ground,
so take care how you tread
when you're barefoot,' she said
as she opened the front of her gown.

The two of them sat on the bed
as she put a hand to her head,
and her conical hat
she put over the cat
she referred to as Tigery Ted,
'that isn't his name though,' she said.

The woman was mellow and moist
her fellow was stiff as a joist,
and she gave him a stroke
(that's the cat not the bloke)
which provided additional hoist.

The two of them soon were entwined
at the middle and up in the mind,
they knitted a spell
and they fitted so well, OK
the seaming was barely defined.

The muddle continued for most
of the night, in the morning the host
said, 'now we're awake
I suggest that we take
a conventional trip to the coast.'

The lovers they went up the lane
made of iron to carry the train
and the nuns at the flat
came and let out the cat
but the broom they secured with a chain.

On the railway the witch was all jolly,
'now, what would you like from the trolley?
It's about to arrive
with a steward called Clive
whose brain is a bit like a cauliflower.'

The witch, she is psychic, you see,
she has visions of things that will be,
but she's not always right
with her visionary sight
which is why she reduces her fee.

When Clive and his trolley appear,
it isn't his brain it's his ear
and the passengers learn
there's a fault in the urn
so its soft drinks or spirits or beer.

The wizard he calls out 'aieeee!'
as Clive drives the bone of his knee
up into his gizzard
upending the wizard
who stupidly asked for a tea.

The train travels over the stones.
The unfortunate customer moans,
the witch is concerned
and the wizard has learned
that the steward has very hard bones.

By the summer the man was in pain
very different from that on the train,
the witch had said 'Rover
the magic is over,'
and he was all tragic again.

He felt like a man on the moon
whose earth is a massive balloon
and he's just seen it burst
and he knows he's the first
and the last.

Chucked

I had taken a pounding.
Love had gone wrong.
More simply, love had gone
and I was not getting over it.
So you took me to your mad mum's
for a North Welsh grounding.
The therapeutic tasks were duly organised
for the taunting pain.
Harvesting the potatoes was the first.
Strenuous, particularly for the unsinuous:
on the edge of my spade.
I found myself on the verge
of my unmade self again.
Second, was the shackling of her shed to a pole:
the ulterior goal,
burying the wood, securing the soul.
And finally, there was taking the dogs
for a run in the sun and the hills.
Exercise to exorcise the haunting.
Some way into the jaunting,
as we sprawled upon the land,
their sandpaper tongues
were rabid upon our cheeks,
weakening my unforgetting,
letting me let go in the sunsetting.
One of them I was to take home
for continuation of the treatment,
the dog, crazy, like her former owner,

kept me on my toes:
busting her legs,
jumping out of car windows,
and snarling up with other dogs
until the only way out
was to pick her up
and throw her away from the fighting,
over a brick wall.
A right naughty little nipper.
A Welsh border liability.
Scampi, in your basket!

My Own Mum

On the ward
you are wearing very thin,
your simple gold ring
is held there by a plaster.
I have come to see you
before my big West End engagement.
I tell you that my name is on the door
with a star above it.
Boasting is best avoided
but under the circumstances
and knowing how you love to hear of my successes,
I lay it on a bit.

It is late afternoon,
you want to know if I am hungry.
I say I will get something later.

You are weakened,
you speak not easily.
Your hospital meal is delivered on a tray.
You signal me to shut the door.
For what I am about to receive
you know the nurse would not be grateful.
You give me the tray,
and motion me to begin.
To the last the meal provider,
to the end the naughty little girl,
always, my Mummy.